Anonymous

Centuries Ago

Songs of Bethlehem

Anonymous

Centuries Ago
Songs of Bethlehem

ISBN/EAN: 9783337264499

Printed in Europe, USA, Canada, Australia, Japan

Cover: Foto ©Lupo / pixelio.de

More available books at **www.hansebooks.com**

Centuries Ago.

SONGS OF BETHLEHEM.

BY VARIOUS AUTHORS.

WITH ARTOTYPE REPRODUCTIONS FROM ADRIAN VAN DER WERFF,
ROGIER VAN DER WEYDEN, AND DOMENICO CHIRLANDAJO.

NEW YORK:

ANSON D. F. RANDOLPH & COMPANY,

900 BROADWAY, COR. 20th STREET.

ILLUSTRATIONS.

FIRST LINES OF THE POEMS.

IT was the calm and silent night !
    Seven hundred years and fifty-three
Had Rome been growing up to might,
    And now was queen of land and sea.
No sound was heard of clashing wars—
    Peace brooded o'er the hushed domain :
Apollo, Pallas, Jove, and Mars
    Held undisturbed their ancient reign.
      In the solemn midnight,
        Centuries ago.

'Twas in the calm and silent night !
    The Senator of haughty Rome,

7

Impatient, urged his chariot's flight,
From lordly revel rolling home ;
Triumphal arches, gleaming, swell
His breast with thoughts of boundless sway;
What recked the Roman what befell
A paltry province far away,
In the solemn midnight,
Centuries ago ?

Within that province far away
Went plodding home a weary boor ;
A streak of light before him lay,
Fallen through a half-shut stable door
Across his path.   He passed—for naught
Told what was going on within ;
How keen the stars, his only thought—
The air how calm and cold and thin,
In the solemn midnight,
Centuries ago !

8

O, strange indifference ! low and high
  Drowsed over common joys and cares ;
The earth was still—but knew not why
  The world was listening, unawares.
How calm a moment may precede
  One that shall thrill the world forever !
To that still moment, none would heed,
  Man's doom *was* linked no more to sever—
    In the solemn midnight,
      Centuries ago !

It is the calm and solemn night !
  A thousand bells ring out and throw
Their joyous peals abroad, and smite
  The darkness—charmed and holy now !
The night that erst no shame had worn,
  To it a happy name is given ;
For in that stable lay, new-born,
  The peaceful Prince of earth and heaven,
    In the solemn midnight,
      Centuries ago !   ALFRED DOMETT.

BEFORE THE PALING OF THE STARS.

Before the paling of the stars,
　　Before the winter morn,
Before the earliest cock-crow,
　　Jesus Christ was born :
Born in a stable,
　　Cradled in a manger ;
In the world His hands had made,
　　Born a stranger.

Priest and king lay fast asleep
　　In Jerusalem ;
Young and old lay fast asleep
　　In crowded Bethlehem ;

Saint and angel, ox and ass,
   Kept a watch together,
Before the Christmas day-break,
   In the winter weather.

Jesus on His mother's breast,
   In the stable cold,
Spotless Lamb of God was He,
   Shepherd of the fold :
Let us kneel with many a maid,
   With Joseph bent and hoary,
With saint and angel, ox and ass,
   To hail the King of glory !

CHRISTINA G. ROSSETTI.

11

THE AIR WAS STILL O'ER BETHLEHEM'S PLAIN.

THE air was still o'er Bethlehem's plain,
  As if the great Night held its breath,
When Life Eternal came to reign
  Over a world of Death.

The Pagan at his midnight board
  Let fall his brimming cup of gold ;
He felt the presence of his Lord
  Before His birth was told.

The temples trembled to their base,
  The idols shuddered as in pain :

12

A priesthood in its power of place
  Knelt to its gods in vain.

All nature felt a thrill divine
  When burst that meteor on the night,
Which, pointing to the Saviour's shrine,
  Proclaimed the new-born light—

Light to the shepherds ! and the star
  Gilded their silent midnight fold—
Light to the Wise Men from afar,
  Bearing their gifts of gold.

Light to a realm of Sin and Grief—
  Light to a world in all its needs—
The Light of life—a new belief
  Rising o'er fallen creeds—

Light on a tangled path of thorns,
  Though leading to a martyr's throne—

A Light to guide till Christ returns
  In glory to His own.

There still it shines, while far abroad
  The Christmas choir sings now, as then,
" Glory, glory unto God !
  Peace and good-will to men !"

14

THERE'S A SONG IN THE AIR!

THERE'S a song in the air !
There's a star in the sky !
There's a mother's deep prayer,
And a baby's low cry !
And the star rains its fire while the Beautiful sing,
For the manger of Bethlehem cradles a King !

There's a tumult of joy
O'er the wonderful birth,
For the Virgin's sweet boy
Is the Lord of the earth.
Ay ! the star rains its fire while the Beautiful sing,
For the manger of Bethlehem cradles a King !

15

In the light of that Star
Lie the ages impearled ;
And that song from afar
Has swept over the world.
Every hearth is aflame, and the Beautiful sing
In the homes of the nations that Jesus is King !

We rejoice in the light,
And we echo the song
That comes down through the night
From the heavenly throng.
Ay ! we shout to the lovely evangel they bring,
And we greet in His cradle our Saviour and King !

J. G. HOLLAND.

16

NIGHT OF WONDER, NIGHT OF GLORY.

Novus rex, nova lex,
Nova natalitia;
Novus dux, nova lux,
Nova fit lætitia.

NIGHT of wonder, night of glory,
　　Night all solemn and serene,
Night of old prophetic story,
　　Such as time has never seen :
Sweetest darkness, safest blue,
That these fair skies ever knew.

Night of beauty, night of gladness,
　　Night of nights—of nights the best :
Not a cloud to speak of sadness,
　　Not a star but sings of rest :

17

Holy midnight, beaming peace,
Never shall thy radiance cease.

Happy city, dearest, fairest,
   Blessèd, blessèd Bethlehem !
Least, yet greatest, noblest, rarest,
   Judah's ever sparkling gem ;
Out of thee there comes the light
That dispelleth all our night.

Now thy King to thee descendeth,
   Borne upon a woman's knee ;
To thy gates His steps He bendeth,
   To the manger cometh He :
David's Lord and David's Son,
This His cradle and His throne.

He, the lowliest of the lowly,
   To our sinful world has come ;

He, the holiest of the holy,
   Can not find a human home.
All for us He yonder lies,
All for us He lives and dies.

Babe of weakness, child of glory,
   At Thy cradle thus we bow ;
Poor and sad Thy earthly story,
   Yet the King of glory Thou :
By all heaven and earth adored,
David's Son and David's Lord.

Light of life, Thou liest yonder,
   Shining in Thy heavenly love ;
Naught from Thee our souls shall sunder,
   Naught from us shall Thee remove.
Take these hearts and let them be
Throne and cradle both to Thee !

HORATIUS BONAR.

"THERE'S A STAR IN THE EAST."

———

" THERE'S a star in the East !" he cried,
    Jasper, the gray, the wise,
To Melchior and to Balthazar
    Up-gazing to the skies.

" Last night from my high tower
    I watched it as it burned,
While all my trembling soul
    In awe and wonder yearned.

" For I know the midnight heavens ;
    I can call the stars by name,—
Orion and royal Ashtaroth
    And Cimah's misty flame.

" I know where Hesper glows,
    And where, with fiery eye,
  Proud Mars in burning splendor leads
    The armies of the sky.

" But never have I seen
    A star that shone like this—
  The star so long foretold
    By sage and seer it is !

" When first I, sleepless, saw it
    Slow breaking through the dark—
  Nay, hear me, Balthazar,
    And thou, O Melchior, hark !—

" When first I saw the star
    It bore the form of a child,
  It held in its hand a sceptre,
    Or the cross of the undefiled.

" Lo ! somewhere on the earth
It shines above His rest—
The Royal One, the Babe,
On mortal mother's breast.

" Now haste we forth to find Him—
To worship at His feet,
To Him of whom the prophets sang,
Bearing oblations meet !"

Then the Three Holy Kings
Went forth in eager haste,
With servants and with camels,
Towards the desert waste.

Ah ! knew they what they bore ?
Gold, for the earthly king—
Frankincense, for the God—
Myrrh, for man's suffering.

With breath of costly spices
And precious gums of Isis,
    The desert air was sweet,
As on they fared by day and night
    Judea's King to greet.

The strange star went before them,
    They followed where it led ;
" 'Twill guide us to His presence,"
    Jasper, the holy, said.

They crossed deep-flowing rivers,
    They climbed the mountains high,
They slept in dreary places
    Under the lonely sky.

One day, where stretched the desert
    Before them far and wide,
They saw a smoke-wreath curling
    A spreading palm beside ;

And from a lowly dwelling
On household cares intent,
A woman gazed upon them,
In mute bewilderment.

" O come with us !" cried Melchior,
And ardent Balthazar,
" We go to find the Christ-child,
Led by yon blazing star !

" Thou knowest how the prophets
His coming long foretold ;
We go to kneel before Him
With gifts of myrrh and gold."

But she, delaying, answered,
" My lords, your words are good,
And I your pious mission
Have gladly understood.

24

" Yet I, ere I can join you,
    Have many things to do :
I must set my house in order,
    Must spin and bake and brew.

" Go ye to find Messiah !
    And when my work is done
I will your footsteps follow,
    Mayhap ere set of sun."

Across the shining desert
    The slow train passed from sight ;
She set her house in order,
    She bleached her linen white.

With busy hands she labored
    Till all at last was done,—
But thrice the moon had risen,
    And thrice the lordly sun !

Then bound she on her sandals,
    Her pilgrim staff she took ;
With bread of wheat and barley,
    And water from the brook ;

And forth she went to find Him—
    The babe Emmanuel,
Who should be born in Bethlehem
    By David's holy well.

All that long day she journeyed ;
    She scanned the desert wide,
In all its lonely reaches
    There was no soul beside—

No track to guide her onward,
    No foot-prints in the sand,
Only the vast, still spaces
    Wide-stretched on either hand !

Night came—but where the Wise Men
    Had seen His burning star,
No glorious sign beheld she
    Clear beaming from afar,

Though Orion and Arcturus
    Shone bright above her head,
And up the heavenly arches
    Proud Mars his legions led !

. . . .

She did not find the Christ-child.
    'Tis said she seeks Him still,
Over the wide earth roaming
    With swift, remorseful will.

Her thin white locks the dew-fall
    Of every clime has wet,—
In palace and in hovel
    She seeks Messiah yet !

27

In every child she fancies
   The Hidden One may be,
On each bright head she gazes
   The mystic crown to see.

She twines the Christmas garlands,
   She lights the Christmas fires,
She leads the joyful carols
   Of all the Christmas choirs;

She feeds the poor and hungry,
   And on her tender breast
She soothes all suffering children
   To softest, sweetest rest.

Attend her, holy Angels!
   Guard her, ye Cherubim!
For whatsoe'er she does for these
   She does it as to Him!

JULIA C. R. DORR.

28

THE MOON THAT NOW IS SHINING.

THE moon that now is shining,
  In skies so blue and bright,
Shone ages since on shepherds,
  Who watched their flocks by night :
There was no sound upon the earth,
  The azure air was still,
The sheep in quiet clusters lay
  Upon the grassy hill.

When lo ! a white-winged angel,
  The watchers stood before,
And told how Christ was born on earth,
  For mortals to adore ;

29

He bade the trembling shepherds
  Listen, nor be afraid,
And told how in a manger
  The glorious Child was laid.

When suddenly in the heavens
  Appeared an angel band,
The while in reverent wonder
  The Syrian shepherds stand ;
And all the bright host chanted
  Words that shall never cease,—
Glory to God in the highest,
  On earth good-will and peace.

The vision in the heavens
  Faded, and all was still ;
And the wondering shepherds left their flocks
  To feed upon the hill :
Towards the blessèd city
  Quickly their course they held,

And in a lowly stable
　　Virgin and child beheld.

Beside an humble manger
　　Was the maiden-mother mild,
And in her arms her son divine,
　　A new-born infant, smiled.
No shade of future sorrow
　　From Calvary then was cast ;
Only the glory was revealed,
　　The suffering was not past.

The Eastern kings before Him knelt,
　　And rarest offerings brought ;
The shepherds worshipped and adored
　　The wonders God had wrought :
They saw the crown for Israel's King,
　　The future's glorious part ;
But all these things the mother kept,
　　And pondered in her heart.

ADELAIDE ANNE PROCTER.

WHILE to Bethlehem we are going,
  Tell me now, to cheer the road,
Tell me why this lovely Infant
  Quitted His divine abode ?
" From that world to bring to this
  Peace, which, of all earthly blisses,
  Is the brightest, purest bliss."

Wherefore from His throne exalted
  Came He on this earth to dwell ;
All His pomp an humble manger,
  All His court a narrow cell ?

32

" From that world to bring to this
    Peace, which, of all earthly blisses,
    Is the brightest, purest bliss."

Why did He, the Lord Eternal,
    Mortal pilgrim deign to be ;
He who fashioned for His glory
    Boundless immortality ?
" From that world to bring to this,
    Peace, which, of all earthly blisses,
    Is the brightest, purest bliss."

Well, then, let us haste to Bethlehem ;
    Thither let us haste and rest ;
For of all Heaven's gifts, the sweetest,
    Sure, is peace—the sweetest, best.

VIOLANTE DO CEO.
Tr. by SIR JOHN BOWRING.

33

GOD REST YOU, MERRY GENTLEMEN.

God rest you, merry gentlemen,
    Let nothing you dismay,
Remember Christ our Saviour
    Was born on Christmas-day ;
To save us all from Satan's power
    When we were gone astray.

In Bethlehem, in Jewry,
    This blessèd Babe was born,
And laid within a manger,
    Upon this blessèd morn ;
The which His mother Mary
    Did nothing take in scorn.

34

From God our heavenly Father,
A blessèd angel came ;
And unto certain shepherds
Brought tidings of the same ;
How that in Bethlehem was born
The Son of God by Name.

" Fear not, then," said the angel,
" Let nothing you affright,
This day is born a Saviour
Of a pure Virgin bright,
To free all those that trust Him
From Satan's power and might."

The shepherds at those tidings
Rejoicèd much in mind,
And left their flocks a-feeding,
In tempest, storm, and wind ;
And went to Bethlehem straightway
The Son of God to find.

And when they came to Bethlehem,
    Where our dear Saviour lay,
They found Him in a manger
    Where oxen feed on hay ;
His mother Mary kneeling down,
    Unto the Lord did pray.

Now to the Lord sing praises,
    All you within this place,
And with true love and brotherhood
    Each other now embrace ;
The holy tide of Christmas
    All other doth efface.

OLD ENGLISH.

36

WELCOME ! THAT STAR IN JUDAH'S SKY.

WELCOME ! that star in Judah's sky,
   That voice o'er Bethlehem's paling glen,
The lamp far sages hailed on high,
   The tones that thrilled the shepherd men :
Glory to God in loftiest heaven,—
   Thus angels smote the echoing chord,—
Glad tidings unto man forgiven ;
   Peace from the presence of the Lord.

The shepherds sought that birth divine ;
   The wise men traced their guided way ;
There, by strange light and mystic sign,
   The God they came to worship lay :

A human babe in beauty smiled,
  Where lowing oxen round Him trod ;
A maiden clasped her awful child,
  Pure offspring of the breath of God.

Those voices from on high are mute ;
  The star the wise men saw is dim ;
But Hope still guides the wanderer's foot,
  And Faith renews the angel-hymn :
Glory to God in loftiest heaven,—
  Touch with glad hand the ancient chord,—
Good tidings unto man forgiven ;
  Peace from the presence of the Lord.

R. S. HAWKER.

38

LIKE SILVER LAMPS IN A DISTANT SHRINE.

LIKE silver lamps in a distant shrine,
    The stars are sparkling clear and bright ;
The bells of the city of God ring out,
    For the Son of Mary was born to-night ;
The gloom is past, and the morn at last
    Is coming with orient light.

Never fell melodies half so sweet
    As those which are filling the skies ;
And never a palace shone half so fair
    As the manger-bed where our Saviour lies ;
No night in the year is half so dear
    As this which has ended our sighs.

The stars of heaven still shine as at first
　　They gleamed on this wonderful night ;
The bells of the city of God peal out,
　　And the angel's song still rings in the height ;
And love still turns where the Godhead burns,
　　Veiled in the flesh from fleshly sight.

Faith sees no longer the stable floor,
　　The pavement of sapphire is there ;
The clear light of heaven streams out to the world,
　　And angels of God are crowding the air ;
And heaven and earth through the spotless birth
　　Are at peace on this night so fair.

W. CHATTERTON DIX.

THE RACE THAT LONG IN DARKNESS PINED.

THE race that long in darkness pined
    Have seen a glorious Light ;
The people dwell in Day, who dwelt
    In Death's surrounding night.

To hail Thy rise, Thou better Sun,
    The gathering nations come,
Joyous as when the reapers bear
    The harvest-treasures home.

For Thou our burden hast removed,
    And quell'd th' oppressor's sway,

Quick as the slaughtered squadrons fell
   In Midian's evil day.

To us a Child of Hope is born,
   To us a Son is given ;
Him shall the tribes of earth obey,
   Him all the hosts of heaven.

His Name shall be the Prince of Peace,
   For evermore adored,
The Wonderful, the Counsellor,
   The great and mighty Lord.

His power increasing still shall spread,
   His reign no end shall know ;
Justice shall guard His throne above,
   And Peace abound below.
                        JOHN MORRISON.

DARK FALLS THE NIGHT, WITHHELD THE DAY.

Dark falls the night, withheld the day,
  Weary we fare perplexed and chill,
Led by one little guiding ray
Shining from centuries far away—
  Good-will and Peace.   Peace and Good-will.

The torch of glory pales and wanes,
  The lamp of love must know decease,
But still o'er far Judean plains
The quenchless star-beam lives and reigns—
  Peace and Good-will.   Good-will and Peace.

And clear to-day as long ago
    The angel-chorus echoes still
Above the clamor and the throe
Of human passion, human woe—
    Good-will and Peace.   Peace and Good-will.

Through eighteen hundred stormy years
    The dear notes ring, and will not cease ;
And past all mists of mortal tears
The guiding star rebukes our fears—
    Peace and Good-will.   Good-will and Peace.

Shine, blessèd star, the night is black,
    Shine, and the heavens with radiance fill,
While on thy slender, guiding track
The angel-voices echo back—
    Good-will and Peace.   Peace and Good-will.

Susan Coolidge.

44

The Holy Night.

The Holy Night.

CHRISTMAS HYMNS AND CAROLS.

SELECTED FROM VARIOUS AUTHORS.

WITH ARTOTYPE REPRODUCTIONS FROM CORREGGIO, FRA ANGELICO,
AND DOMENICO ZAMPIERI.

NEW YORK:

ANSON D. F. RANDOLPH & COMPANY,

900 BROADWAY, COR. 20th STREET.

ILLUSTRATIONS.

FIRST LINES OF THE POEMS.

ALL HAIL, THOU NIGHT, THAN DAY MORE BRIGHT

ALL hail, thou night, than day more bright,
    Through whose mysterious shade,
In wondrous birth, arose on earth,
    From bosom of pure Maid ;
The Sun new-born, a Star of morn,
    Filling the world with light !

He, who alone, from heaven's high throne,
    Rules all, and doth restore
To God's embrace man's fallen race,
    Lies on a cottage floor ;
Like Him that we, save poverty,
    Have nought to call our own.

7

While o'er their sheep close watch they keep,
　Those shepherds first receive
The heavenly call, that doth to all
　Great joy and gladness give,—
The call from heaven, to watchmen given
　That wake and never sleep.

From the Amiens Breviary.
Tr. by W. J. BLEW.

8

WHEN CHRIST WAS BORN OF MARY FREE.

WHEN Christ was born of Mary free,
In Bethlehem, that fair citie,
Angels sang there with mirth and glee,
   "In excelsis gloria."

Herdsmen beheld these angels bright,
To them appearing with great light,
Who said, "God's Son is born to-night,
   In excelsis gloria."

The King is come to save mankind,
As in Scripture truths we find,
Therefore this song we have in mind,
   "In excelsis gloria."

9

Then, dearest Lord, for Thy great grace,
Grant us in bliss to see Thy face,
That we may sing to Thy solace,
    " In excelsis gloria."

Harleian MSS.

ALL THIS NIGHT BRIGHT ANGELS SING.

ALL this night bright angels sing,
Never was such carolling.
Hark! a voice which loudly cries:
"Mortals, mortals, wake and rise;
    Lo, to gladness
    Turns your sadness;
From the earth is ris'n a Sun,
Shines all night, though day be done."

Wake, O earth, wake everything,
Wake and hear the joy I bring;
Wake and joy; for all this night
Heaven and every twinkling light,
    All amazing,
    Still stand gazing;

Angels, Powers, and all that be,
Wake, and joy this Sun to see.

Hail, O Sun, O blessèd Light,
Sent into this world by night,
Let Thy rays and heavenly Powers
Shine in these dark souls of ours ;
    For most duly
    Thou art truly
God and man, we do confess ;
Hail, O Sun of Righteousness !

WILLIAM AUSTIN.

12

GOOD NEWS FROM HEAVEN THE ANGELS BRING.

Good news from heaven the angels bring,
Glad tidings to the earth they sing ;
To us this day a child is given,
To crown us with the joy of heaven.

This is the Christ, our God and Lord,
Who in all need shall aid afford ;
He will Himself our Saviour be,
From sin and sorrow set us free.

To us that blessedness He brings,
Which from the Father's bounty springs ;
That in the heavenly realm we may
With Him enjoy eternal day.

All hail, Thou noble Guest, this morn,
Whose love did not the sinner scorn!
In my distress Thou cam'st to me:
What thanks shall I return to Thee?

Were earth a thousand times as fair,
Beset with gold and jewels rare,
She yet were far too poor to be
A narrow cradle, Lord, for Thee.

Ah, dearest Jesus, Holy Child!
Make Thee a bed, soft, undefiled,
Within my heart, that it may be
A quiet chamber kept for Thee.

Praise God upon His heavenly throne,
Who gave to us His only Son;
For this His hosts, on joyful wing,
A blest New Year of mercy sing.

From the German of Martin Luther.

14

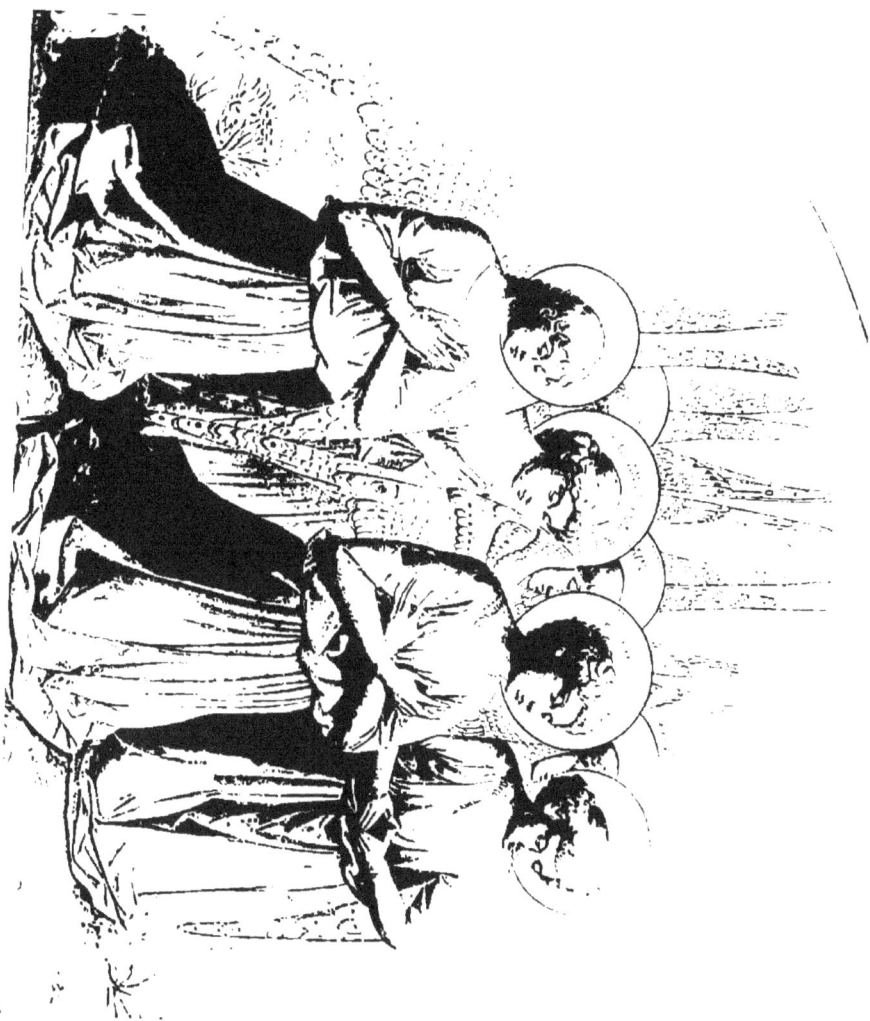

A CHILD IS BORN IN BETHLEHEM.

A CHILD is born in Bethlehem ;
Rejoice and sing, Jerusalem.
Within a manger He doth lie,
Whose throne is set above the sky.
    Hallelujah ! hallelujah !

The wise men came, led by the star ;
Gold, myrrh, and incense brought from far.
The ox and ass beheld that sight,
The creature knew the Lord of might.
    Hallelujah ! hallelujah !

His mother is the Virgin mild,
And He the Father's only child.

The serpent's wound He beareth not,
Yet takes our blood and shares our lot.
   Hallelujah ! hallelujah !

Our human flesh He enters in,
Yet free from every stain of sin.
To fallen man Himself He bowed,
That He might lift us up to God.
   Hallelujah ! hallelujah !

On this most blessèd jubilee,
All glory be, O God, to Thee !
O Holy Three, we Thee adore,
This day, henceforth, forevermore.
   Hallelujah ! hallelujah !

From the Latin, Fourteenth century.

A GREAT AND MIGHTY WONDER.

A GREAT and mighty wonder
　The festal makes secure :
The Virgin bears the Infant
　With Virgin-honor pure.

The Word is made incarnate,
　And yet remains on high ;
And cherubim sing anthems
　To shepherds from the sky.

And we with them triumphant,
　Repeat the hymn again :
"To God on high be glory,
　And peace on earth to men ! "

While thus they praise your Monarch,
Those bright angelic bands,
Rejoice, ye vales and mountains!
Ye oceans, clap your hands!

Since all He came to ransom
By all be He adored,
The Infant born in Bethlehem,
The Saviour and the Lord!

And idol forms shall perish,
And error shall decay :
And Christ shall wield His sceptre,
One Lord and God for aye.

From the Greek of Anatolius.

Tr. by Rev. John Mason Neale.

18

OF THE FATHER'S LOVE BEGOTTEN.

Of the Father's love begotten,
　　Ere the worlds began to be,
He is Alpha and Omega,
　　He the source, the ending He,
Of the things that are, that have been,
　　And that future years shall see,
　　　Evermore and evermore !

He is here, whom seers in old time
　　Chanted of, while ages ran ;
Whom the voices of the Prophets
　　Promised since the world began ;
Then foretold, now manifested,
　　To receive the praise of man,
　　　Evermore and evermore !

19

Oh, that ever-blessèd birthday
　　When the Virgin full of grace,
Of the Holy Ghost incarnate
　　Bore the Saviour of our race ;
And that Child, the world's Redeemer,
　　First displayed His Sacred Face,
　　　　Evermore and evermore !

Praise Him, O ye heaven of heavens !
　　Praise Him, angels in the height !
Every power and every virtue
　　Sing the praise of God aright !
Let no tongue of man be silent,
　　Let each heart and voice unite,
　　　　Evermore and evermore !

Thee let age, and Thee let manhood,
　　Thee let choirs of infants sing ;
Thee the matrons and the virgins,
　　And the children answering ;

Let their modest song re-echo,
   And the heart its praises bring,
     Evermore and evermore !

Laud and honor to the Father !
Laud and honor to the Son !
Laud and honor to the Spirit !
   Ever three and ever one :
Consubstantial, co-eternal,
   While unending ages run,
     Evermore and evermore !

From the Latin of Prudentius.

SLEEP, HOLY BABE.

"But see the Virgin blest
Hath laid her Babe to rest."—MILTON.

SLEEP, Holy Babe,
    Upon Thy mother's breast :
Great Lord of earth and sea and sky,
How sweet it is to see Thee lie
    In such a place of rest !

Sleep, Holy Babe :
    Thine angels watch around,
All bending low, with folded wings,
Before the Incarnate King of kings,
    In reverent awe profound.

Sleep, Holy Babe,
  While I with Mary gaze
In joy upon that face awhile,
Upon the loving Infant smile,
  Which there divinely plays.

Sleep, Holy Babe :
  Ah ! take Thy brief repose :
Too quickly will Thy slumbers break,
And Thou to lengthened pains awake,
  That death alone shall close.

Then must those hands,
  Which now so fair I see,
Those little pearly feet of Thine,
So soft, so delicately fine,
  Be pierced and rent for me.

Then must that brow
  Its thorny crown receive ;

That cheek, more lovely than the rose,
Be drenched with blood, and marred with
blows,
That I thereby may live.

Rev. Edward Caswall.

24

WHY, MOST HIGHEST, ART THOU LYING.

Why, most Highest, art Thou lying
   In a manger poor and low ?
Thou, the fires of heaven supplying,
   Come a stable's cold to know ?

     O, what works of love stupendous,
       Were salvation's price !
     Burning wert Thou to befriend us,
       Exiles far from Paradise !

On a mother's breast Thou sleepest,
   Mother, yet a Virgin still ;
Sad, with eyes bedimmed Thou weepest,
   Eyes which heaven with gladness fill.

O, what works of love stupendous,
   Were salvation's price !
Burning wert Thou to befriend us,
   Exiles far from Paradise !

Weak, the Strong, of strength the Giver ;
   Small, whose arms creation span ;
Bound, who only can deliver ;
   Born is He who ne'er began.

O, what works of love stupendous,
   Were salvation's price !
Burning wert Thou to befriend us,
   Exiles far from Paradise !

From the Latin.

CHRISTIANS, AWAKE, SALUTE THE HAPPY MORN.

CHRISTIANS, awake, salute the happy morn,
Whereon the Saviour of mankind was born;
Rise to adore the mystery of His love
Which hosts of angels chanted from above;
With them the joyful tidings first begun
Of God incarnate and the Virgin's Son.

Then to the watchful shepherds it was told,
Who heard the angelic herald's voice: " Behold,
I bring good tidings of a Saviour's birth
To you and all the nations upon earth:
This day has God fulfill'd His promised word,
This day is born a Saviour, Christ the Lord."

27

He spake; and straightway the celestial choir
In hymns of joy, unknown before, conspire:
The praises of redeeming love they sang,
And heaven's whole arch with alleluiahs rang;
God's highest glory was their anthem still,
Peace upon earth, and unto men good-will.

To Bethlehem straight the happy shepherds ran,
To see the wonder God had wrought for man:
And found with Joseph and the blessèd maid,
Her Son, the Saviour, in a manger laid:
Amazed, the wondrous story they proclaim,
The earliest heralds of the Saviour's Name.

Let us, like those good shepherds, then employ
Our grateful voices to proclaim the joy:
Trace we the Babe, who hath retrieved our loss,
From His poor manger to His bitter Cross;
Treading His steps, assisted by His grace,
Till man's first heavenly state again takes place.

Then may we hope, the angelic thrones among,
To sing redeemed, a glad triumphal song ;
He, that was born upon this joyful day,
Around us all His glory shall display ;
Saved by His love, incessant we shall sing
Eternal praise to heaven's Almighty King.

JOHN BYROM.

29

WAKE, ALL MUSIC'S MAGIC POWERS.

WAKE, all music's magic powers
  On this blissful morning,
Born to-day, the Child is ours,
  Theme of prophets' warning :
Giant in the race He towers,
  Toil and danger scorning.
O, that blessèd going out
Which salvation brought about !

, Let this glorious holiday
  Find such holy spending
That the simple-hearted may
  Joy without offending,
And sweet charity may stay,
  With our concourse blending.
30

O, that blessèd going out
Which salvation brought about !

O, how bright is this day made,
    Day with radiance glowing,
Which the Light of light displayed,
    Light in darkness showing !
Chasing thus death's gloomy shade,
    Brightness o'er us throwing !
O, that blessèd going out
Which salvation brought about !

Risen to-day in splendor bright,
    Shining to all ages,
Beams the Sun, whose distant light
    Touched the Prophet's pages ;
Now, to end the reign of night,
    Christ His power engages.
O, that blessèd going out
Which salvation brought about !

From the Latin.

CAROL, BROTHERS, CAROL.

CAROL, brothers, carol,
   Carol joyfully :
Carol the good tidings,
   Carol merrily ;
And pray a gladsome Christmas
   For all good Christian men.
Carol, brothers, carol,
   Christmas times again.

Carol ye with gladness,
   Not in songs of earth ;
On the Saviour's birthday,
   Hallowed be our mirth.
While a thousand blessings
   Fill our hearts with glee,

Christmas-day we'll keep, the
  Feast of Charity !

At the joyous table
  Think of those who've none,—
The orphan and the widow,
  Hungry and alone.
Bountiful your offerings
  To the altar bring ;
Let the poor and needy
  Christmas carols sing.

Listening angel music,
  Discord sure must cease ;
Who dares hate his brother
  On this day of peace ?
While the heavens are telling
  To mankind good-will,
Only love and kindness
  Every bosom fill.

Let our hearts responding
    To the seraph band
Wish this morning's sunshine
    Bright in every land !
Word and deed and prayer
    Speed the grateful sound,
Bidding merry Christmas
    All the world around.

34

COME, YE LOFTY! COME, YE LOWLY!

COME, ye lofty! come, ye lowly!
  Let your songs of gladness ring!
In a stable lies the Holy,
  In a manger rests the King:
See, in Mary's arms reposing,
  Christ by highest heavens adored:
Come! your circle round Him closing,
  Pious hearts that love the Lord.

Come, ye poor! no pomp of station
  Robes the Child your hearts adore:
He, the Lord of all salvation,
  Shares your want, is weak and poor:
Oxen round about behold them,
  Rafters naked, cold and bare:

See! the shepherds! God has told them
That the Prince of Life lies there.

Come, ye children, blithe and merry!
This one Child your model make;
Christmas holly, leaf and berry,
All be praised for His dear sake:
Come, ye gentle hearts and tender!
Come, ye spirits keen and bold!
All in all your homage render,
Weak and mighty, young and old.

High above a star is shining,
And the Wise Men haste from far:
Come, glad hearts, and spirits pining!
For you all has risen the Star.
Let us bring our poor oblations,
Thanks and love and faith and praise;
Come, ye people! come, ye nations!
All in all draw nigh to gaze.

Hark ! the heaven of heavens is ringing :
    Christ the Lord to man is born :
Are not all our hearts, too, singing
    Welcome, welcome, Christmas morn ?
Still the Child, all power possessing,
    Smiles as through the ages past,
And the song of Christmas-blessing
    Sweetly sinks to rest at last.

ARCHER GURNEY.

JOY AND GLADNESS.

———————

Joy and gladness! joy and gladness!
    O happy day!
Every thought of sin and sadness
    Chase, chase away.
Heard ye not the angels telling,
Christ the Lord of might excelling,
On the earth with man is dwelling,
    Clad in our clay?

With the shepherd throng about Him
    Haste we to bow:
By the angel's sign they found Him,
    We know Him now;

New-born Babe of houseless stranger,
Cradled low in Bethlehem's manger,
Saviour from our sin and danger,
    Jesus, 'tis Thou !

God of Life, in mortal weakness,
    Hail, Virgin-born !
Infinite in lowly meekness,
    Thou wilt not scorn ;
Though all heaven is singing o'er Thee,
And gray wisdom bows before Thee,
When our youthful hearts adore Thee,
    This holy morn.

Son of Mary, (blessèd mother !)
    Thy love we claim ;
Son of God, our elder brother,
    (O gentle Name !)

To Thy Father's throne ascended,
With Thine own His glory blended,
Thou art, all Thy trials ended,
    Ever the same.

Thou wert born to tears and sorrows,
    Pilgrim divine ;
Watchful nights and weary morrows,
    Brother, were Thine :
By Thy fight with strong temptation,
By Thy cup of tribulation,
O Thou God of our salvation,
    With mercy shine !

In Thy holy footsteps treading,
    Guide, lest we stray ;
From Thy word of promise shedding
    Light on our way :

Never leave us nor forsake us,
Like Thyself in mercy make us,
And at last to glory take us,
    Jesus, we pray.

THE BABE IN BETHLEHEM'S MANGER LAID.

The Babe in Bethlehem's manger laid,
 In humble form so low ;
By wondering angels is surveyed,
 Through all His scenes of woe.
Nöel ! Nöel !
Now sing a Saviour's birth !
All hail ! all hail !
His coming down to earth !

A Saviour ! sinners all around
 Sing, shout the wondrous word ;
Let every bosom hail the sound,
 A Saviour ! Christ the Lord !
Nöel ! Nöel !
Now sing a Saviour's birth !

All hail ! all hail !
His coming down to earth !

For not to sit on David's throne
   With worldly pomp and joy ;
He came for sinners to atone,
   And Satan to destroy.
      Nöel ! Nöel !
   Now sing a Saviour's birth !
   All hail ! all hail !
   His coming down to earth !

To preach the Word of Life divine,
   And feed with living Bread,
To heal the sick with hand benign,
   And raise to life the dead.
      Nöel ! Nöel !
   Now sing a Saviour's birth !
   All hail ! all hail !
   His coming down to earth !

He preached, He suffered, bled and died,
　Uplift 'twixt earth and skies ;
In sinner's stead was crucified,
　For sin a sacrifice.
　　　Nöel ! Nöel !
　　Now sing a Saviour's birth !
　　　All hail ! all hail !
　　His coming down to earth !

Well may we sing a Saviour's birth,
　Who need the grace so given ;
And hail His coming down to earth
　Who raises us to heaven.
　　　Nöel ! Nöel !
　　Now sing a Saviour's birth !
　　　All hail ! all hail !
　　His coming down to earth !

Old French.

44

www.ingramcontent.com/pod-product-compliance
Lightning Source LLC
Chambersburg PA
CBHW032238080426
42735CB00008B/902